Michael Peters

Nov. 22, 1989

The Best Way to
PLAN YOUR DAY

DAYTON
AND
ENGSTROM

POCKET GUIDES
Tyndale House Publishers, Inc.
Wheaton, Illinois

Unless otherwise noted, Scripture quotations are from the *Holy Bible,*
King James Version.

Adapted from *Strategy for Living* by Edward R. Dayton and Ted W.
Engstrom, copyright 1976 by Regal Books. Used by permission.

First printing, April 1989
Library of Congress Catalog Card Number 89-50080
ISBN 0-8423-0373-1

CONTENTS

Goals Can Change Your Day!

The world is continually offering us choices. The futurists of our day tell us that we are suffering from over-choice. There are just too many decisions to make each day. We become confused.

"What model of car shall I buy? What options should it have? Would it be better to buy a used car or a new one?"

"What dress should I buy? Will the style change?"

"Where should my children go to school?"

"Where should we live?"

"Is this the right job for me?"

"Where shall we eat dinner tonight?"

All of this is the result of living in an affluent Western society. The farmer scratching out a living in a village in India faces no such problems. His goal is very clear. He wants to survive. And that clear goal keeps him pushing on.

He wakes up each morning knowing exactly what steps he has to take to accomplish that goal. Passersby may offer interruptions. His children may be looking for attention. There may be a big political rally in the next village. But that Indian farmer will not be distracted. His goal is set, his priorities are clear, and his plans are made.

GOALS ARE MOTIVATORS

Goals are one of the most powerful motivating forces known to people. Psychiatrist Dr. Ari Kiev of Cornell Medical Center states, "With goals people can overcome confusion and conflict over incompatible values, contradictory desires, and frustrated relationships with friends and relatives, all of which often result from the absence of rational life strategies.

"Observing the lives of people who have mastered adversity, I have repeatedly noted that they have established goals and, irrespective of obstacles, sought with all their effort to achieve them. From the moment they've fixed an objective in their mind and decide to concentrate all their energies on a specific goal, they begin to surmount the most difficult odds."[1]

We have all seen this, haven't we? Wilma Rudolph, for example, overcame the crippling effects of childhood polio to win her dream: gold medals in the 1960 Olympic 100- and 200-meter races. Billy Graham has become the world's leading evangelist because he focused on what it was he wanted to do and moved toward that goal with God-given determination.

Goals have the power to lift our eyes from the mud below toward the sky above. They are statements about what could be, what should be, what can be. They are statements of faith.

WE ALL HAVE GOALS

In one sense, we all have goals. We may not be aware of them, but they are there. God has placed in us basic drives that motivate us toward certain types of goals. Psychologist Abraham Maslow described these inner motivators as a "hierarchy of needs."[2]

At the very foundation of our being are *physiological* needs. We must have food and water merely to stay alive. When we are dying of thirst, our entire attention is focused on one goal: Get water!

At a higher level, there are needs for *safety* and *security*. When we are alone on a

MASLOW'S HIERARCHY OF NEEDS

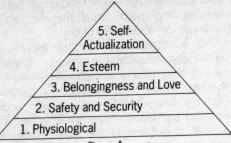

5. Self-Actualization

4. Esteem

3. Belongingness and Love

2. Safety and Security

1. Physiological

Figure A

deserted city street at midnight, our primary goal is to arrive home safely.

Once these needs are met we can then turn our thoughts to *loving* and *being loved* and feeling as though we are a part of the group. We set goals to deepen friendships or to care for our children.

One step higher on the scale is *esteem,* the need for self-respect, a feeling of self-worth. To have high self-esteem is to feel good about being you.[3]

At the top of Maslow's hierarchy is the need for what he calls *self-actualization.* By self-actualization Maslow means we should become so free we are no longer concerned with self. Maslow visualizes the self-actualized person finding his self-actualization in giving himself away to others.

Whether we recognize it or not, we all have assumed goals at each one of these levels. In our prosperous Western societies, few of us have concern for hunger and thirst. Our goals are concerned with needs of self-esteem, belongingness, and wanting to love and be loved.

But if tomorrow an airplane in which we are flying crashes on a desert island, our concern—and thus our goals—will immediately move to the more basic level—the need to survive. Yet there also may come a time in our life when we will knowingly bypass one level of need for a higher one.

Goals, then, are primary motivators for life. If we understand our goals, we will better understand our life. If *we change our goals, we change our life.*

☞ Checkpoint

Complete the following sentences:
1. My greatest goal in life is to . . .
2. Five years from now I would like to have . . .
3. By the end of this year I hope that I will have . . .
4. This week I hope to . . .
5. Today I hope to . . .

WHY ARE SOME PEOPLE AFRAID OF GOALS?

Probably the greatest fear we have of setting goals is the fear of failure. Somehow we feel that if we have made a statement about something we are going to do or something we are going to accomplish, and we don't do it or accomplish it, we will have become a lesser person. Others will not regard us as highly as they did before. (There is some truth in this. If we continually fail, people will conclude that we are a failure.)

People respond to this fear in some interesting ways. Some people set their goals so high they are always impossible to meet. "Let's shoot to have 500 people at church next week!" Or, "Let's increase sales by 200 percent next year." The goal is so high that everyone understands it won't be met.

Others consistently set their goals low enough so they're always sure of success. "Suppose we plan on having seventy-five people here next week." Or, "We'll just be glad to keep the same number of orders coming in."

There is a way out of this tension. The most effective people are those who set their goals just beyond what they can reasonably expect of themselves. "They set moderately difficult, but potentially achievable, goals. In biology, this is known as the *overload principle*. In weight lifting, for example, strength cannot be increased by tasks that are performed easily or that cannot be performed without stress to the organism. Strength can be increased by lifting weights that are difficult, but realistic enough to stretch the muscles."[4]

GOALS VS. PURPOSES

What about setting goals for life? How do
we go about it? Where do we begin? First,
we need to understand a few terms.

When a baseball player stands up at the
plate, his goal is very clear and measurable. His goal is not to be a "good ball
player." At that moment in time his goal is
to get a base hit.

His goal is *measurable*. It is *accomplishable*. He will know when he has done it or
failed to do it. And he is not afraid of
failure. He knows that even the best
ballplayer fails to get a hit more than six
out of every ten times at bat.

A parent needs to have measurable
goals. "In order to be a better father, I intend to spend four hours playing ball with
my son every Saturday morning." We
have no way of being sure that spending
those four hours will really produce a
more effective father. But we do have a
clear statement of intentions.

A *goal* is a future event that we believe

11

is both accomplishable and measurable in terms of what is to be done and how long it takes to do it.

A *purpose,* on the other hand, is an aim or direction, something we want to achieve, but something that is not necessarily measurable.

To be a great mountain climber is a "purpose." To climb Pike's Peak during the month of January is a "goal." To purchase all the climbing gear necessary to climb Pike's Peak by December may or may not be a goal, depending on whether "all the climbing gear necessary" is well established. It may be better to say, "Purchase climbing shoes, backpack, and canteen by December."

WELL-WRITTEN GOALS

Stated in terms of end results.

Achievable in a definite time.

Definite as to what is expected.

Practical and feasible.

Precisely stated in terms of quantities, where applicable.

Limited to one important goal or statement.

Figure B

To use another illustration, goals are the bricks with which purposes are built. The goals come in all shapes and sizes and fit together to build the chief purposes of our lives. Individually, daily goals may seem small, even inconsequential. But together our goals make us what we are and what we intend to be.[5]

HOW TO WRITE GOOD GOALS
One way to get this distinction in perspective is to attempt to write a few goals and notice the difference between goals and purposes. But before you try, look at the characteristics of well written goals and poorly written goals in Figure B.

POORLY WRITTEN GOALS
Stated in terms of process or activities.
Not fully achievable; no specific target dates.
Ambiguous as to what is expected.
Theoretical or idealistic.
Too brief and indefinite or too long and complex.
Written with two or more goals per statement.

If you find that you have difficulty in writing a goal for a particular purpose, try breaking the goal down into its various parts—or sub-goals—and writing goals for each of these. In this way, you will still get what you want—a definable, measurable, accomplishable goal.

To go back to the illustration of trying to be an effective father, we may find that in order to realize our purpose of being an effective father, we have to list a number of goals. These might be (1) to spend four hours each Saturday morning playing ball with my son; (2) to make sure that at least fifteen minutes of the discussion around the dinner table is centered on the activities of our children; (3) to have a weekly planning session to decide on what TV programs we will watch.

We could diagram it something like Figure C.

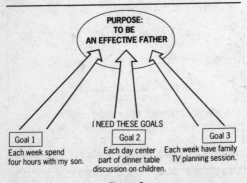

PURPOSE: TO BE AN EFFECTIVE FATHER

I NEED THESE GOALS

| Goal 1 | Goal 2 | Goal 3 |

Each week spend four hours with my son.

Each day center part of dinner table discussion on children.

Each week have family TV planning session.

Figure C

RELATING GOALS TO ONE ANOTHER

In the same way that all of our actions intertwine so do our goals. There are big ones and little ones, some that should happen very soon and some that are far away. Some goals are dependent upon others.

Let us use a golf game as an illustration. My long-range goal for the golf game is to have a lower total score than any of my opponents. However, my long-range goal is really the summation of a series of intermediate goals—my score for each hole. Each of these is made up of some immediate goals, such as the goal of sinking a fifteen-foot putt.

All of these goals are not only related in time, but they also depend on one another. I can't move on to reaching a goal of completing the second hole until I have met my goal of completing the first hole. And so it goes.

"All right," you say. "I've got that. I can see how it really would be great if I had some clear idea of what I wanted to do and to be. Having measurable goals sounds good. But how do I do it?"

SEVEN STEPS TO SETTING GOALS

Step 1: Understand your purpose. What is it that you would like to do or to become? What is the general direction toward which you would like to move? Make a statement about that.

Step 2: Picture the situation. Imagine

the situation not as it is now, but as you would like it to be. What does it look like? Who are you with? What are you doing? What are the circumstances?

Step 3: State some long-range goals. What measurable and accomplishable events would have to happen in order for that purpose to be realized?

Step 4: State your immediate goals. What are the things that you have to accomplish today if you are going to move toward your ultimate purpose?

Step 5: Act. Pick out one of the goals and start moving toward it. Remember that every long journey begins with the first step!

Step 6: Act as if . . . Act as if you have already reached your goal. If you are going to start working toward that first goal, you have to start acting as if you have really reached it. How does it impact all the other parts of your life? How does it affect your plans for your job, your family, others? This may help you uncover some other goals that you need to consider.

Step 7: Pray. If you are going to live life with a sense of lasting purpose, then you need to ask for God's direction in all of this.

Notice that the steps to uncover goals move from the future backward to the present. This is the way we plan. When we go to carry out our plans we move in the opposite direction.

TOMORROW'S GOALS
IMPACT TODAY

Setting goals not only helps us to think about what we should do today, but it also forces us to anticipate the results of our present actions. So it has both long-range and short-range benefits.

Suppose, for example, that you as a husband are frustrated by your inability to relate to your family when you come home from work. You arrive home tired, full of the problems of the day and anticipating the difficulties of tomorrow. Your mind is far away from your family, and your family knows it. You would like to relate to your children, but somehow it just doesn't seem to fit together.

Let us see, then, how the seven steps might work in practical situation just outlined. Let's try this goal-setting process on a reasonably short-range basis. Suppose your purpose is "improving things at home on weekday evenings."

Step 1: Understand your purpose. Let's say you would like to have evenings at home that have less tension and have a feeling of the family being more together.

Step 2: Picture the situation. What kind of a situation would you like to find when you are home from the office? Imagine the ideal situation. How are you relating to your family? How are they relating to you? What are you saying to one another? What needs of your family can you meet? What are the needs you have that they can meet?

Step 3: Set long-range goals. Set some specific goals for how things could be in your family, say, six months from now. Perhaps you would like to have a weekly family time. What would each member of the family have to do to help reach the goal of having a good time together?

Step 4: Set short-range goals. A pastor attending one of our seminars, who has faced this same situation, suggests that you set this short-range goal: As you drive home from the office, take time to focus on the needs of each member of your family. Take time to think about the things they are going to be talking about and needing to hear from you. Get emotionally prepared for them.

While that may be an immediate, short-range goal for you, perhaps your wife needs the goal of planning and preparing the evening meal before you arrive home (assuming she doesn't work) so she is free to be with you and the children. Perhaps the children's schedules need to be changed around so they are more open and available. Perhaps a better solution would be for you to spend an hour alone with your wife when you first arrive home so you are really ready to enter into the children's activities after suppertime.

Step 5: Act. Pick one of these goals and go to work on it immediately. How about setting a goal to have considered each member's needs by the time you arrive home?

Step 6: Act as if . . . If you are going to change your thinking this evening, you should be acting that way through the day. Maybe this means that, as you head for your car, you have to start acting as if things are going to be all right at home that evening.

Step 7: Pray. Perhaps in the midst of this God will show you a better way.

The point is that by describing the situation as you would like to have it, you can take steps and make decisions now as to how you might arrive at that goal.

Most of us know that we need to "plan ahead." What we often fail to realize is that if we don't set specific daily and weekly goals, we really have nothing to plan ahead for.

IT'S A PROCESS

There is more to living a purposeful life than just setting goals. We need to find ways to analyze our present commitments and situations and to see ourselves as whole persons.

We need to somehow find ways to live an integrated life.

We need to discover what our value system is and then find ways to work this all through. We will discuss these things in the following chapters. The important thing is to understand that we have more control over our futures than most of us tend to believe.

☞ Checkpoint

For you. Think about a purpose you would like to work on. Using the seven steps we have suggested, decide what action you would have to take today to move toward that purpose.

For you and your spouse. Decide together on a purpose you both would like to work toward and then independently go through the seven steps. After you have done this, compare the goals you and your spouse have listed. Where do they differ and why do they differ?

What would be needed to come up with a set of goals to which you both agree? There is a simple saying: "Good goals are *my* goals. Bad goals are your goals."

Make sure your goals are *our* goals!

For you and your family. Lead your children through this same exercise. Pick something they would like to do. Let them think of any way-out idea that comes up. After they have utilized all their fantasies to state the general situation they would like to be in someday, lead them backward from the future into the present. You will be surprised at what good goals they may suggest!

CHAPTER 2

How to Set Priorities That Stick

Goals, priorities, and planning—these are the steps to move you toward living a purposeful life. We have talked about *goals,* what they are and what they are not. We suggested steps to coming up with some good goals. But how will you know which are the best goals?

WHEN WE NEED PRIORITIES
We need to sort out our priorities when we have more goals than we can handle.

21

We need to sort out our priorities because the world keeps changing.

We need to sort out our priorities to decide what to do next.

You can have too many goals. If you sat down and made a list of all the goals it might be nice to have, the list would be endless. Get a new job? Take a trip to Hawaii? Spend Christmas with the family? Join the choir? Learn to play golf?

The world keeps changing. Things are never the way they should be. They very seldom are the way we plan them to be. Consequently, there will always be a need to rejuggle our priorities, to sort things out afresh.

What to do next? In one sense all priority questions are "when" questions. We are trying to decide what to do next and what to do after that. The least important things we will never get around to.

CHOOSE THE FUTURE

Over the entrance of the Archives Building in Washington, D.C., is the phrase "What is past is prologue." The past can have a fascination for us. But phrases like "We've always done it this way" or "We tried that and it didn't work" can be deadly in considering a new goal.

Too often we become enmeshed in pursuing a goal that was appropriate five, ten, or twenty years ago, but is meaningless today. So our first question might be: *Is this just a goal out of the past? Does it really have to do with the future?*

PRIORITY QUESTIONS

The following are some other questions you can ask about your goals that will help you sort out your priorities:

How urgent is it? When must it be done? Right now? Today? Soon? Someday?

General Eisenhower is quoted as saying, "The urgent is seldom important, and the important is seldom urgent." Too often life is controlled by the "tyranny of the urgent." We put aside higher and more worthy goals to put out fires.

The trouble is, many of us enjoy putting out fires. "Fire fighting" can become a major purpose in our lives. It distracts us from some of the other difficulties we need to face further along the road. And it gives us a wonderful excuse to move along with the tide of circumstances.

We have all met fire fighters, haven't we? They have a breathless urgency about them. There is a large problem out there that only they can handle.

There are probably fire fighters in your church, your shop, your office, your family. Maybe you are one!

How important is it? Very important? Quite important? Somewhat important? Not so important?

This question of importance will force us back to our reasons for setting the goal in the first place. What is the *why* of it?

Not everything we do can be important. But some things should be. There are great chunks of life that are routine and somewhat monotonous. But if we're doing nothing that is important to us, we will soon conclude—perhaps rightfully so—that we are unimportant people.

How often must it be done? Is it something we have to do daily? Weekly? Occasionally? Sometime? Perhaps not at all?

There are some things we need to do regularly. They are the little molehills that will become mountains if they are not tended to on a timely basis. It may be a small thing—like eating—but if we don't do it regularly, the rest of life will end.

Can someone else do it more effectively than I? Perhaps the answer is no. Or, again, it could be maybe. If the answer is yes, then perhaps this shouldn't be one of your goals at all. However, this introduces the whole area of delegation, a subject outside the scope of this book.[1]

Is it part of the larger task to which I am committed? This question relates our specific goals to our higher purpose. In his book *The Systems Approach,* C. West Churchman describes how necessary it is to ask the question, "Of what higher system is this system a part?"[2]

In other words, what is the big picture? What is the meaning of it all? Only God can give the ultimate answer to that question.

We should expect to find that our goals are related to a higher purpose. If we picture all of our goals in relationship to higher goals and purposes, we will discover that life becomes much more a whole.

Ask the question: *What will happen if it is not done at all?* Will there be a disaster? Trouble? Difficulty? Nothing? If the answer is nothing, maybe that's a clue to give it a low priority.

The American approach to problems is summed up in the proverb, "Never put off until tomorrow what you can do today." Europeans seem to take quite the opposite approach. Their view might be summed up, "Put off everything you can until tomorrow, for tomorrow you might not have to do it."

Both views, at various times, are undoubtedly correct! We need to decide which fits now.

Last, ask the question: *Is this the best way?* Is there a better goal that needs to be substituted for this one?

Suppose you have a goal to have everyone available four times to practice a Christmas program. But on reflection you see that it could be broken down into three subgroup rehearsals of the choir, the actors, and the reader. It's a much better way. And easier to manage as well.

When we discuss personal planning, we

25

will have more to say about considering alternate solutions and thus finding optimum solutions.

PUTTING IT TOGETHER—THE ABCS

How does this fit together? What might be a procedure that you could use to establish priorities for your different goals? Which goals come first? Which goals are more important?

Start by making a list of all the goals that you have considered. The list doesn't have to be in any particular order, but sometimes it is helpful to put your goals down in logical groups.

One way of grouping them would be by goals that have to do with relationships to others and goals that had to do with tasks. Some people like to make a list of all the things they would like to be and another of all the things they would like to do.

The result may be a very long list of goals. And there is nothing more frustrating or discouraging than to be presented with a long list of items and being asked to rank them in value, say, one through 100. The mind just can't hold all the information.

Besides, you are comparing each item with the other ninety-nine. And as soon as you have identified one goal as being number one, it automatically means that all the rest are less than one. And life doesn't work that way, does it?

There is no reason why we have to have one goal that is our top priority. We are much more likely to have a number of goals, all of which we consider "number one."

So, how do we handle such a long list?

There is a simple and effective way of sorting things out in terms of priorities. It has been around a long time and is surprisingly simple. It's called the ABC *technique.* Instead of trying to assign each goal a ranking number, assign it a value, an "A," "B," or "C."

A = "Must do" or very high value

B = "Should do" or medium value

C = "Can do" or low value

You can use the ABC technique in one of two ways. The first way is to go down your list and decide which of these goals you consider to be A goals. If it's a B or C, go right past it. Just mark A's.

Now go back to the list and decide which ones are B goals. The rest are automatically Cs.

A second way is to pause at each goal and decide whether you think it is an A, B, or a C.

It does not matter which of these methods you use. Some people find one easier than the other.

Now go back and look at your list. If you had a very long list, you may discover that you have too many A goals. We used to tell people to forget all those Bs and Cs because they would not have time for them. But then one of our friends put A next to all of his!

If you have too many A goals, then use the same ABC technique for all the A's. Ask the ABC question not in terms of all your goals, but just of these A goals. Subdivide the A goals into A-a, A-b, and A-c.

You can see that what we are doing here is continually narrowing down the field. If you kept the process up, theoretically you would eventually arrive at just one. A goal. It really works very nicely.

If you think about it, we do our ABCs all the time. It is very much like Maslow's hierarchy of needs. As we sit on an airplane headed for home over Christmas holidays, our A priority may be to be with our family. If the aircraft crashes on the way, we may immediately shift to a new A, survival.

What we are doing here is recognizing this continuous process and consciously putting it to work.

Take a little time now and test out this idea. You will find it useful in making all kinds of decisions.

PRIORITIES HAVE TO DO WITH VALUES

The goals we choose and the priorities we give to them are a reflection of our values or what we call a value system. But what is a value system? When asked to describe our value system, most of us feel some-

☞ Checkpoint

For you and your family. Have each member of the family make a list of the purposes of your family life. Combine them all into one large list. Now have the family group go through the list using the ABC technique to establish areas of agreement or disagreement on what are the major purposes of your family.

You can do this in one of two ways. Have each member individually rank all of the goals in terms of ABC, then compare lists and discuss them. Or, you can take an oral vote on each one as you go along, assigning an A only to those on which the entire family is agreed.

what embarrassed. We recognize that we should have such a system, but we have probably never been asked to describe it.

Our real value system is reflected by what we do, not what we believe. What we believe may eventually change what we do, but for the moment our actions reflect our value system.

How can you discover your own value system? In their excellent book, *Values Clarification,* the authors point out that the best way to discover your values is to give yourself a number of choices and see which ones you would prefer.[3]

You might write down all of your purposes in life and then use the ABC technique to decide which of these you would place at the top of the list. By then asking yourself why you have given high priority to some items and low priority to others, you can get in touch with your real motivators, your real values.

WHAT MAKES A "CHRISTIAN" VALUE SYSTEM?

A value system that is distinctly Christian must have its roots in the authority of God's Word. Christians can look to the Bible to discover the basis for deciding which things should come first in life.[4]

We believe the Bible gives people three broad levels of priority:

First, commitment to God and Christ;

Second, commitment to the Church, which the Bible calls the body of Christ;

Third, commitment to the work of Christ.

Level One. Jesus said that there is no way to God except through Him. (See John 14:6.) He said that those who believe that He is the Christ are given the power to become God's sons and daughters. (See John 1:12.) He puts commitment to Himself higher than any other possible relationship. (See Matt. 10:37-39.)

Level Two. The Bible gives us few direct measurements of commitment. But one that we hear over and over is this: The real measure of Christianity is our love for each other. Jesus thought this was important enough to call it a new commandment. "A new commandment I give unto you, that ye love one another" (John 13:34). "This is how all men will know that you are my disciples, because you have such love for one another" (John 13:35, Phillips).

Jesus came to change relationships. He came first to change the relationship between the individual and the Father. But He always assumes that the outworking of this renewed fellowship is also going to result in a new kind of relationship between all those who name His Father as their Father.

Level Three. What is the "work of Christ"?

One way of thinking about this priority is to compare the two major tasks of the Church. The first of these is what we have come to call "nurture,"—building up people for ministry. (See Eph. 4:11-12.) The other part of the work of the Church is to "go forth"—to evangelize, to visit those in prison, to care for widows, to give a cup of cold water in Jesus' name, to have compassion upon the hungry and the poor.

How will the work get done? As we build our relationships within the Church, on the strong foundation of our relationship to God in Christ, we will discover that there is a natural base on which we can do the work of Christ. (See Figure A.)

Some will immediately object, pointing

31

out that if we spend all of our time relating to one another, we may never get around to doing the work of Christ. They are right. A struggle must always go on.[5]

Perhaps St. Augustine summed the matter up best when he said, "Love God and do as you please." If we love the Lord with all our mind and all our body and all our strength and our neighbor as ourselves, there is little doubt that what we want to do will be what Christ wants us to do.

If you haven't made a commitment to God and Christ, make it now! If you have, recognize that this commitment has brought you into a new relationship, not only with the Father, but with those who call themselves Christians. Center your purpose and goals in these two relationships and with these as a foundation, move on to doing His work.

WHAT ABOUT THE REST OF MY LIFE?
"Well, that's fine," you may say. "But what about all the rest of my life? Do these three priorities cover everything?"

| 3. Work of Christ |
| 2. Body of Christ |
| 1. Commitment to Christ |

Figure A

No, they don't. There is a great deal of living to do that may be very difficult to fit into these three priorities. The grass needs to be mowed, the dishes need to be washed, we need to earn a living. But as we try to align our total life purpose and the goals that issue forth from that purpose in a God-ward direction, we need some way to sort all this out. We will discuss the practical working out of this kind of priority system in the next chapter, which covers planning.[6]

☞ **Checkpoint**

Take a look at your datebook for the last week or mentally review what you did during the week. Where does it appear that your top priorities really lie?

CHAPTER 3

The Best Way to Plan

PLANNING SAVES TIME

How strange it is that many of us who recognize the crucial need for planning in our church, business, or profession never apply planning concepts to our personal life. For in the same way that planning saves time (and a great deal of money and energy) in an organization, so it will save time for us. Within obvious limits, there is a direct relationship between the amount of time we spend planning and our effectiveness in reaching our goals. (See Figure A.)

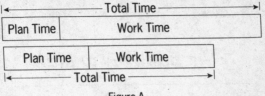

Figure A

We experience this every day: "If I had only thought to bring that tool, this job would be a cinch." "Why didn't I remember I had to take Jimmy for a haircut? Now I will have to make two trips." "Why Mabel, I thought *you* were bringing the lunch!"

Many people think they don't have time for planning. They tend to be activists, people who want to get on with it. But if there is no planning, then we will probably do the first thing that comes to our minds whether it is effective or not. The most effective people are those who have trained themselves to think (plan) before they act. If someone rushes in with a "We've only got ten minutes to . . . ," your best response is, "OK, let's take three minutes to plan."

WHAT IS PLANNING?
Planning is trying to discover how to accomplish our goals. There may be many ways to reach the goal. The question

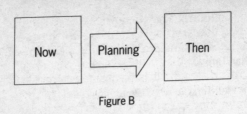

Figure B

before us is what is the best way.

Planning is moving from the "now" to the "then," from the way things are to the way we want them to be. Like goals, plans are statements of faith, for they have to do with the future.

In Figure B we have shown planning as an arrow. It points in a direction. It is a road map toward the future, a map that we can constantly improve as we move toward that future.

It's a way of thinking about the future before the future happens. Notice we said that it is a way of *thinking* about the future. That's the nice thing about planning; we can imagine what the future is going to be like and take those steps that will be more likely to give us satisfaction and less likely to give us dissatisfaction.

PLANS ARE CHANGEABLE
But let's face it, some people do not like to plan. One of the reasons some people dislike "planning" is they conceive it as making a rigid and predetermined set of decisions as to what they are going to do

in the future. They believe a plan is something that *must* be carried out. Or they become so enamored with their plans they can't give them up. As the writer of Proverbs said, "It is pleasant to see plans develop. That is why fools refuse to give them up even when they are wrong" (Prov. 13:19, TLB).

Plans, whether they are personal plans or organizational plans, should always make provision for continuous evaluation. We should plan, take the first step, look back (get feedback) and look forward, and reevaluate what is going on. If the plan is still good, fine. If it is not, let's change it.

We find this kind of feedback in almost everything we do in daily life. Yet some planning we do so automatically that we don't even realize we are doing it. For example, as we are driving an automobile from our home to the store, we are continuously planning. From the moment we set out to reach the store—our goal—and we decide on the route we will take—our plan—we are constantly reevaluating on the basis of the situations we face.

Some situations, such as an unexpected pothole in the road, require an instant change of plan—a quick jerk of the steering wheel. Others, such as an accident at an intersection that is backing up traffic, cause us to make a more calculated change of plan and take a different route to the store. Of course, we don't expect to change our big plans from moment to moment, but we should expect that they will change, for the future is seldom like we expect it to be.

PLANS HELP COMMUNICATE
Planning helps us move toward goals, but planning helps in many other ways as well. Planning is a way of communicating our intentions to ourselves and to others. "Can two walk together, except they be agreed?" (Amos 3:3). Unless you have decided where you are going, how can I decide to accompany you?

PLANNING IS LIKE
PROBLEM SOLVING
Planning is a way of seeking alternate and thus optimum solutions to reaching our goal or solving a problem. In this sense, planning is very much like problem solving. We assume that we can reach the goal; we also assume that just as there are many roads that may lead to our destination, so there might be many ways in which we could reach our goal. Knowing that something will not work is just as valuable as knowing what will work. Better to "fail" on paper than in practice.[1]

We need to plan, but we need to see planning as a tool, not as an end in itself. There is a tension about plans. Some people love to plan. We can get so wrapped up in planning (which is basically

☞ **Checkpoint**

List five goals that you have for which you have no plans. These might include everything from having dinner ready at six o'clock to making a big business decision. Note which of these might be more likely to happen if you had a plan.

thinking about tomorrow) that we do not live today. Somehow the tension between being a "today person" and a "tomorrow person" needs to be continually worked on. It's never resolved.

HOW TO DO PERSONAL PLANNING

When making plans, you have to start with a goal. If you don't know where you're going, any road will take you there. What is it that you want to do or to be? Picture the situation as you want it to be.

It may be that you will have to start with a purpose and then break it down into goals, all of which may contribute toward that one purpose. It may even be—as we will see later—that you have to make a plan to plan.

Next, describe as best you can the situation as you understand it. There are two specific factors in your present situation you might want to consider: the forces *helping* and the forces *hindering* the situation.

In his "force field analysis," Kurt Lewin suggests that seeing a situation in the light of helping and hindering forces is an excellent way to analyze a problem.[2]

We agree.

To see how all this works, let's look at the two examples in the planning form in Figure C.

THE CASE OF THE LONELY HUSBAND

Roger Jensen had a new goal: He wanted to spend two hours a week alone with his wife. It was part of his larger purpose to be a more effective husband. He decided that as part of this purpose he wanted to have

---

PLANNING WORKSHEET

Step 2 Present Situation	Step 3 Forces Helping
Reading 4 or 5 books	Desire to do a better job.
	Forces Hindering
	No regular program No specific reading goals. T.V. news-papers. Not enough time. Read too slow

Figure C

more quality time with her. So he wrote down in the right-hand column: "To spend two hours a week alone with my wife, beginning next week." (See Figure C.)

He then set about analyzing his present situation in the left-hand column: "We don't seem to have enough uninterrupted time to share where we're at." He noted under "Forces Helping" that he had a desire to be with her. Then under "Forces Hindering" he noted that the kids kept interrupting them, they had conflicting schedules, and there just didn't seem to be enough time.

With this information in hand, Roger started working through steps toward his goal. His first step was to "discover what

Step 4 **Steps to Goal**	Step 1 **My Goal**
1. Decide on types of books I want to read. 2. Estimate number of pages in twenty books. 3. Estimate my reading speed. 4. Figure out time needed. 5. Decide on most optimum block of time. 6. Set aside time. Protect it. _or_ Think of times to use that are now wasted.	To read twenty books this year.

she would like." That's a pretty good idea. Certainly if they were going to have some quality time together, they ought to know what kind of time it should be. Next, he decided to make some specific dates on the calendar and protect them in advance.

But Roger knew very well that his past history indicated he often didn't keep all the appointments he made, so he wrote down, "3. Ask secretary for help." This was a wise move. We all need to hold ourselves accountable for the things we want to do, and by asking his secretary to remind him of his weekly date with his wife—which for Roger and his wife, Mary, was a weekly luncheon together—he took a final step toward making his goal a habit.

THE CASE OF THE "CRASH COURSE" MANAGER

Bud Barnes was a manager in a middle-sized engineering firm. He had been promoted because of technical ability, but he discovered that there was a great deal to be learned about this business of management that he had not been taught in college.

As he thought through his long-range goals, one of his shorter-range supporting goals turned out to be that he should read twenty management books during the coming year. He pulled out his sheet of paper and wrote his reading goal on the right-hand side. (See Figure C.)

Then he began to take a look at his present situation. As best he could tell he was reading no more than four or five books of all kinds in one year.

When he looked for "Forces Helping" him to move toward his goal, he knew that he had a desire to do a better job. The "Forces Hindering" seemed to be that he had no regular reading program, no specific reading goals. TV and newspapers kept taking up his time. He also concluded that he was a slow reader. What could he do?

Bud started working on some steps toward the goal. Like Roger Jensen, he recognized that the first step he had to take was to analyze exactly what it was he wanted to do, what type of books he wanted to read. He decided that after he had compiled such a list, a second step would be to estimate the number of pages in those twenty books. A third step for Bud was to estimate his reading speed. This in turn led him to step four, which was to find out how much time he was going to need to read all of those pages.

For the moment he put aside the idea of trying to learn to read faster.[3]

Instead, he planned to take step five and block out some optimum reading time. The final step of his plan was to put this time down on his calendar and to protect it and to think of other ways he might fit in reading time during the week.

THE CASE OF THE CONCERNED MOTHER

Clare Johnson had a personal problem. Her fifteen-year-old daughter, Christy, was going through a counterdependent stage in her life. What had, up until a few months ago, been a close relationship between mother and daughter was now becoming more and more strained.

Clare's immediate problem was that she was concerned with Christy's dating habits. Christy had announced that she had a big date with a friend by the name of Alan next Saturday night, and she wanted permission to stay out until two in the morning.

As Clare thought about her problem, she asked herself, "What goals are involved here? What is it I really want for Christy?"

She knew that her purpose in her relationship with Christy was to help her make her own decisions and become a mature person. Clare also recognized that she had another purpose: As a mother she wanted to maintain communication with her daughter, to be a restraining influence as well as an encouraging influence where it was needed. As she thought about these two purposes, she concluded that her goal was to make sure Christy would understand her concern. If at all possible she wanted to let Christy make her own decisions.

What were some of the alternatives? Clare could forbid Christy to go, but that would really only solve the immediate problem. She could insist that she talk to Alan's mother first, but that would make Christy feel more like a child than an adult. She could plan conflicting family programs for the same date. But that would be both dishonest to herself and to Christy.

Finally, Clare took out a sheet of paper and worked out the plan shown in Figure D. The means she used to communicate with Christy was an "I-message." "Christy, if you did not come home until two o'clock on Sunday morning, I know that I would feel very upset. I really don't know Alan, and you've never stayed out past twelve before. What can you do to help me?"[4]

Clare hoped that her daughter would offer an alternative solution and from this they might work out an arrangement with which they were both happy. If the alternative solution was not acceptable, Clare would have to rest in the hope that Christy would feel more loved because her mother was exercising her judgment and authority.

Roger, Bud, and Clare—we've shown you three examples of working out a planning sheet. But that's still not the whole process. After you do a planning sheet, you still need to ask two very important questions.

45

IS IT PRACTICAL?

Once you have arrived at what appears to be a good plan in terms of steps to be taken, the final question is, "Is it practical?" You need to calculate the amount of time, money, and effort that will be needed for each step. Only after you have added up the total resources needed, and have ascertained that they are indeed available, do you have a workable plan.

Suppose your ideas don't add up? Perhaps they cost too much or are just impractical, and you discover you have a plan that won't work. Don't be discouraged. Even with failures you can make valuable progress.

Thomas Edison worked long and hard

PLANNING WORKSHEET

Step 2 Present Situation	Step 3 Forces Helping
1. Christy wants to go out with Alan, stay out until 12 o'clock 2. Don't know Al	Christy's growing need for independence **Forces Hindering** Christy never stayed out after 12 o'clock before

Figure D

in his laboratory doing experiment after experiment in an attempt to find the right filament for the incandescent electric light. On a particular day he had just completed his ten thousandth experiment only to discover another way that wouldn't work. When he arrived home from his laboratory that night, he shared this bit of news with his wife.

"Aren't you pretty discouraged, Tom?" she asked.

"Discouraged?" responded Edison. "Certainly not! I now know 10,000 ways that won't work!"

Experimenting on paper can save a lot of work in the laboratory of life. Better to fail in the planning than in the execution.

Step 4 **Steps to Goal**	Step 1 **My Goal**
1. Under what circumstances would I be willing to have Christy stay out until 2 o'clock. 2. Sort out my own feelings so that I can express my problem and recall an "I message." 3. Share my concern with Christy and my need to be reassured of her well-being. 4. Make a decision.	Purpose 1. Maintain communication with Christy. 2. Be a restraining influence as well as encouraging influence. GOAL Help Christy to make a decision acceptable to Alan and Christy.

Your first plan (or plans) can lead you to alternative plans that will succeed. As you find alternatives, you will reach your goal or solve your problem.

WHERE DO YOU GET ALTERNATIVE PLANS?

Someone has aptly noted that the cleanliness of theory is no match for the mess of reality. If we start doing our planning within the context of where we are right now, we may soon give up.

Somehow we have to take our mind away from the negative situation at hand and draw from both our experience and the experience of others all of the different ideas that may be there. If you're stuck in some quicksand, there is little use in analyzing its consistency. Better to look for a nearby branch!

For the moment, we need to ignore the problem of the present and consider the possibilities of the future. There are a number of ways of doing this:

The Random List. Some people prefer to sit down with a blank sheet and just list out all the ideas that come to them in any random fashion. Then they go back and try to order these in some logical way, eliminating the ones that won't work.

The Slip Technique. Others find that the *slip technique* works well. On a batch of three-by-five cards or—less expensive!—slips of paper, write down every idea you have. Pay no attention to logic or what has gone before. Later on, spread these written ideas out on a table and arrange them in ways that will work into a usable plan.

This process has the double benefit of showing gaps in thinking, gaps that can prompt us to identify new ways of filling in missing steps. This approach also works very well as a brainstorming technique with other people, say, the members of your own family.

Here's an example. A family is planning a vacation. Suppose they sit down around the dining room table, each one with a small pile of slips in front of him.

Dad might say, "All right, what is it we want to get out of this vacation?"

Junior might reply, "Learn to water ski!"

To which Dad might respond, "Fine, write that down!" And with this Junior could write down his idea on his own slip of paper.

"What else do we want to get out of this vacation?"

"Well, I'm hoping for a good rest from cooking," Mother might reply.

"Fine, write that down!" should be Dad's response. As each person goes through thinking of all the things he/she might want on the vacation and writes down his/her ideas, the family will probably discover that they are building on each other's ideas and can eventually plan a vacation that is acceptable to them all. Or, as an alternative, they can do it one way this year with the promise of doing it another way next year.

You can use this technique for idea gathering whether you're planning a vacation, thinking about your honeymoon, or listing characteristics of the kind of person you would like to become. The secret is to take every idea as it comes, without judgment and—hopefully—without comment, then do your evaluating later.

PLAN TIME TO PLAN

Planning does take time, but it's worth it. We need to set aside time to plan on our calendars, or we may never get into the habit of doing it.

How often should you plan? In terms of reviewing your life goals, you should replan at least once a year. Goals and plans that lie a year ahead should probably be reviewed every three months. Monthly plans should be reviewed each week. And then there are the daily plans.

USE A "THINGS-TO-DO" LIST

No one seems to have come up with a better way of managing the minutia of life than making a daily "Things-to-Do" list—a random list of all the things you plan to do this day. By noting in one place everything you have to do, you get a picture of your whole day.

A "Things-to-Do" list helps integrate your different daily needs. You can group some things such as telephone calls or note that you can combine a trip to the market with a trip to pick up the kids at school. You can remember birthdays that need a friendly greeting and, generally, lay out the progress of life.

But if making a list is going to become a habit, it must first get down on your calendar. So plan ten minutes for it at the beginning or end of each day, a half hour at the end of each week, perhaps two hours each month.

This approach to planning—the making of lists—is useful in planning for both big goals and smaller ones. You will soon discover that big plans lead to the need for smaller plans. For example, when working on a big plan for a new career you should first list all the major steps. These major steps can then in themselves become goals for which you can make more detailed, smaller plans.

Pray about your plans. For the Christian, thoughtful, personal planning and devotional time are linked very closely. Don't be surprised if in the midst of your praying you are suddenly struck with a new solution to a nagging problem or another alternative for the future. "A man's mind plans his way, but the Lord directs his steps" (Prov. 16:9, RSV). Expect that the Holy Spirit is going to put into your mind alternatives for better goals.

☞ **Checkpoint**

For you. From the planning worksheet examples in this chapter, make your own copy of the form and try filling it in with your own plan. Choose some goal with which you are very familiar. It may even be one you have already achieved. In the "goal" column write down a clear goal statement, one that is accomplishable and measurable. In the proper columns, state the "Present Situation," "Forces Helping," and "Forces Hindering." Now attempt to write down the steps needed to reach the goal. Do this for a number of different areas for your life.

For your family. As a family or as husband and wife, choose a goal for which you would like to plan. Write it in the "goal" column. In the left-hand column write down what you believe the situation to be and next gather the information—perhaps using the slip technique—to write down the "Forces Helping" or "Forces Hindering." Use the slip technique to gather ideas on all of the steps that might take you toward the plan.

Now sort out the most useful ideas and write a plan. For each step of the plan estimate the date when it can be accomplished. Estimate the cost and time for taking each step.

Calculate whether this is a practical plan. If it doesn't seem practical or costs too much, be glad! You now know one way that won't work. Go back and try another alternative.

CHAPTER 4

Living Life to the Full

Any discussion about goal setting and establishing priorities that deals with only one portion of our daily life is bound to fail. We cannot separate that which we do at the office from that which we do at home, or that which we do with our children from that which we do at church. Life is a whole. Activity in each area will impact on every other. Those who attempt to live a compartmentalized life are continually forced to juggle their priorities. They end up being one person in one situation and another person in another situation.

PICTURE THE WHOLE PERSON

But how different we all are! Of the some 8 billion people who have lived, no two have ever been completely alike, not even identical twins. What a fantastic concept!

Each one of us is shaped by a different *history,* lives in a different *situation,* has different *commitments* and obligations, and has different needs and *goals.* We might picture ourselves as being in the center of our history, our present situation, our present commitments, and our future goals (Figure A).

In this diagram we have tried to picture the four dimensions that affect us all. These dimensions make each of our lives so different. We have purposely drawn our diagram so that the person in the center can be seen as suspended between his or her personal history, commitment, situation, and future goals.

By *history* we mean such things as past education, ethnic background, experience,

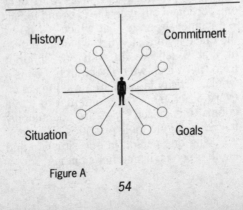

Figure A

and a host of other things that have happened to you in your own or your parents' past. What is the sum of your history? What are all of the things in your past that have made you what you are today?

There is nothing you can do about your history. What has happened has happened—you cannot change the past. If, for example, you grew up with a poor education, there is nothing you can do to change that fact. But you can make plans to get more and better training.[1]

Our present *situation* is comprised of such things as our age, our marital status, the job we have, the titles we carry, the place we live, the language we speak—or don't speak. Some of these things can be changed. Others cannot.

Our *commitments* are those things we believe are related to our dedication to life and to others. We have commitments to our employer, commitments to our employees, commitments to our colleagues and friends. On a more mundane level, we have commitments to the local bank and other lending institutions!

Our *goals* are our hopes for the future, our statements of faith about what we want the future to be like. Notice in our diagram that if we take away the goals, we are immediately pulled back into past history and strung out between our commitments and our present situation.

How many different areas of life there are! In the Life Areas Worksheet (Figure

LIFE AREAS WORKSHEET

Areas	Commitments
God	
Spouse	
Children	
Relatives	
Friends	
Business Associates	
Others	
Learning	
Relaxation	
Recreation	
Hobbies	
Physical Well-being	
Emotional Well-being	
Spiritual Well-being	
Occupation	
Employer	
Finances	
Service to God	
Service to the Church	
Service to Humanity	
Educational Achievement	
Technical Achievement	
Social Achievement	
Financial Achievement	
Career Achievement	
Spiritual Achievement	
Acquisition of Things	
Home	
Car	
Clothes	
Future	
Parenthood	
Retirement	

Situation	Goals

Figure B

B), we have listed some of them. We have purposely put three columns after the list of life areas to help you consider those life areas to which you have a commitment, those that reflect your general situation, or those for which you have or should have goals.

Go down the list. Add other items to it. You are a special person in a special situation. You need to see the whole person, a person made up of all of the different aspects of your life.

To be a whole person is (1) to understand who you are, where you have come from, what your present commitments are and (2) to have a clear picture of where you believe God wants you to move.

By including in our thinking all our present commitments and our entire present situation, and by not compartmentalizing life into such things as work, family, leisure, and so forth, we are able to integrate our goals. The better job of integration we do, the more effective we will become as persons.

THINGS ARE AS THEY ARE

It is a trite but very true statement: Things are as they are. To put it another way, you are as you are. You cannot do much about your history, but you can understand your present commitments and your present situation. This understanding will help you discover whether your goals are realistic and whether you have included among them all of the things you need to do.

How can you discover if your goals match up with your present situation? Go through these six steps:

1. Analyze your present commitments.

2. See how you perceive you are spending your time.

3. Take an actual inventory of how you spend your time daily.

4. Look at your calendar of appointments (if you keep one).

5. Compare your goals against your present commitments, your perception of how you spend your time, your time inventory, and your appointment calendar.

6. Restate your list of goals as needed.

To help you see how all this works, consider the example of Bill, a thirty-year-old engineer who has a wife and two small children. We made a list of goals for Bill (Figure C) and we have also worked out some simple forms that take him through the six steps outlined above.

As you go through Bill's example, you may want to evaluate your own goals to see if they are practical and realistic. But remember, if you are not quite ready to do all these exercises, don't let that stop you. Finish the chapter and come back to these six steps later, perhaps even after finishing the book.

PRESENT COMMITMENTS

First, analyze your present commitments: jobs, assignments, committee responsibilities, bills, debts, and so forth. In Figure D we've filled out the form as Bill might have done. Note that the form includes personal and family commitments.

Make your own form, and use Bill's example to list as many of your own commitments as you can. These might include family, job, finances, hobbies, friends, causes to which you are committed—anything for which and to which you believe you have a commitment. If you would like a little help to prime the pump on listing commitments, look again at the Life Areas Worksheet (Figure B).

BILL'S GOALS

1. To spend an average of one half hour each day in personal prayer and Bible study.
2. To save $10,000 during the next four years for the children's education.
3. To receive a Master of Engineering degree two years from next June.
4. To spend one hour a week alone with each of the children.
5. To move from my present job into a similar job in the field of energy conservation by January 1.
6. To have a two-day vacation alone with Betty by the end of next month.
7. To serve the church in an underdeveloped country for a period of at least two years when I am between the ages of fifty and fifty-five.
8. To increase our family charitable giving to 20 percent of our gross income by the end of next year.

Figure C

After each commitment listed, indicate whether it is personal—yours alone—or whether it is jointly shared by you and other members of your family. A personal commitment might be a commitment to your wife or, on a much smaller scale, your agreement to serve on a church committee. A shared commitment might be one that you and your wife or family have toward your local church or, at a more mundane level, the promissory note you both signed when you borrowed money from the bank to pay for the family car.

BILL'S COMMITMENTS

Commitment	Personal	Family
My wife, Betty	X	
Trinity church		X
$1,000 loan to United Bank	X	
Complete the Alpha Project by June 1	X	
Neighborhood collection for Heart Fund next month	X	
Weekly breakfast with Bill Jones	X	
Funds for kids' education		X
Monthly car payment of $92		X
Board of Orange Street mission	X	
Taking Billy to the park each week	X	
Reading and praying with Nancy before bed nightly	X	
Tennis club membership and weekly matches	X	

Figure D

Why look at our commitments? For one thing, some of them cannot change. There are certain givens, such as your commitment to your husband or wife, that cannot be revoked. Winston Churchill is quoted as saying, "It's not enough that we do our best; sometimes we have to do what's required." On the other hand, many commitments will eventually be discharged so that we can move on to new things.

An excellent way of gaining some insight is to have another member of your family (your spouse, if you are married) fill out a sheet for you. Have them list those things they believe you are committed to. If you are married, you also might want to have your spouse fill out the same kind of sheet for himself or herself so that you can review your commitments together.

Warning: This can lead to some surprising and sometimes disturbing insights. You may discover that you are committed to quite different things or you may discover that what you thought was a family commitment was really one to which only you are committed.

HOW ARE YOU SPENDING
YOUR TIME?

The next step is to perceive how you are spending your time. In Figure E you can see how Bill did it. Use the example to make an evaluation of your own time and how you are spending it. List anything that comes to mind—at home, with your business, with your family, in your spiritual life—anything at all.

As you move along, or after you have completed the list, evaluate each item. What do you think about this particular time investment? Do you believe that for the area you have listed you are spending too little time, just the right amount of time, or too much time?

BILL'S PERCEPTION OF HIS TIME

How Am I Spending My Time? Note anything that comes to mind: home, business, family, spiritual life, etc.	Too Little	Just Right	Too Much
Business meetings			X
Church Board			X
Personal devotions	X		
Time with Betty	X		
Work interruption			X
Driving to work			X
Watching TV			X
Woodworking hobby	X		
Playing with kids	X		
Prayer group	X		
Professional education	X		
Reading the newspaper		X	
Sleeping		X	
Eating	X		
Leisure	X		
Planning	X		

Figure E

WHAT DOES YOUR TIME INVENTORY SAY?

Next comes the most difficult assignment of all—one that is used in many areas of organizational life, but one that is hard to carry out. We suggest that for an entire week you keep track of everything you do, using fifteen-minute increments, from the time you wake up until the time you go to bed. In order to carry out such an assignment, you may need help from your family or fellow workers. See Figure F for a sample of how Bill kept a time inventory for a week. Then make up your own form with enough spaces for a week, and make a real effort to fill it in every day.

When you have finished the week, you probably won't believe the results. "I just couldn't have spent that much time doing *that!*" you may decide. Both of us go through this exercise about once a year. That's about all we can stand, for even with the best intentions none of us do what we think we will do. So all the more reason to try it once and see for yourself. But don't be discouraged. Remember the baseball player who feels success when he hits four times out of ten at bat.

LOOK AT YOUR APPOINTMENTS

The last step is to take a close look at your appointment book or calendar for the past month. Figure G shows you one week of

BILL'S DAILY TIME INVENTORY

	Monday	Tuesday
7:00	awoke and dressed	
7:30	Breakfast read Together	
8:00	Drive to office	
8:30	Look over mail sort for replys	
9:00	worked on Johnson project	
9:30	Read technical mag.	
10:00	called Johnson coffee break	
10:30	Johnson project	
11:00		
11:30	↓	
12:00	Lunch with Abe	
12:30		
1:00	↓	
1:30	talked to secretary	
2:00	phone calls talked to Res B	
2:30	↓	
3:00	Worked on Johnson coffee break	
3:30	Johnson project	
4:00	answered mail	
4:30	Talked to Boss	
5:00	Drove home	
5:30	Read newspaper	
6:00	had dinner	
6:30	Read newspaper	
7:00	Drove to meeting	
7:30	Board meeting	
8:00		
8:30	↓	
9:00	drove home	
9:30		
10:00	Talked to wife Went to sleep	

Figure F

ONE WEEK FROM
BILL'S APPOINTMENT BOOK

Monday	Friday
12:15 Lunch with Abe 7:30 Church Board	6:30 Dinner with Rogers

Tuesday	Saturday
7:30 Breakfast with Sam	9:00 Little League practice 8:00 Date with Betty

Wednesday	Sunday
12:30 Lunch with Betty 7:00 Choir practice	1:30 Platts for dinner

Thursday	
8:30 Project presentation to department head 8:00 Bible Study Group	

Figure G

Bill's. If you don't have a regular appointment book or calendar, reconstruct the past month as best you can.

COMPARING GOALS TO PRACTICE

Review your list of goals and make sure each one is numbered as in Bill's sample in Figure C. The numbers do not signify any special priority system; they are simply a way of identifying each goal.

Now comes the moment of truth! Review each of the four sheets you have completed: time commitments, perception of how time is spent, daily time inventory, and appointment book. Next to any entry on each sheet put the identification number(s) of any goal you feel might be associated with that entry. To see how Bill, our hypothetical engineer, did it, see Figures H and I. Note the several things Bill did that were not associated with his goals. Then try the same exercise yourself. You will probably discover that your batting average just about matches Bill's.

ANALYZING THE RESULTS

Go back over your worksheets again. Look at the items that apparently have nothing to do with your goals. Why did you do those things that were not associated with your goals? Which were just time wasters? Why were they time wasters? What could you have done about

them? Could they have been eliminated? Could they have been delegated to someone else who could have done them just as well? Or does there begin to emerge from all of this some hidden goals, goals that you really have had all along and want to continue to keep?

Look over the things on which you feel you spent too much time. Were they things you wanted to do or things somebody else wanted you to do? Review the things on which you spent too little time. Again, were they things you wanted to do or things others wanted you to do?

What do the answers to these questions tell you about what is directing your life? Again we suggest that you may want to do this with a member of your family or your spouse by having them fill out their perception of how you are spending your time. This will give you an idea of how others perceive you.

REBUILD YOUR GOALS
In light of this analysis, decide which goals now seem less important, which should be eliminated, and what new ones should be added. It could very well be that from this study you will see quite a different set of priorities than the ones you thought you had. See Figure J for how Bill revised his goals in light of his analysis.

As we said at the beginning of this chapter, going through these steps takes time and effort, but it does pay off because it helps you face reality. On one hand you have your goals, your description of the way you would like things to be. On the other hand, you now have a description of how things really are. Your situation is very much like the one we talked about in the chapter on planning. You have a *now* and a *then*. (See Figure K.)

BILL'S REVISED GOALS

1. To spend an average of one half hour each day in personal prayer and Bible study.
2. To save $10,000 during the next four years for the children's education.
3. To receive a Master of Engineering degree two years from next June.
4. To spend one hour a week alone with each of the children.
5. To move from my present job into a similar job in the field of energy conservation by January 1.
6. Have two-day vacation alone with Betty by the end of next week.
7. To serve the church in an underdeveloped country for a period of at least two years when I am between the ages of fifty and fifty-five.
8. To increase our family giving to 20 percent of our gross income by the end of next year.
9. To train effective replacement for church board by December 31.

Figure J

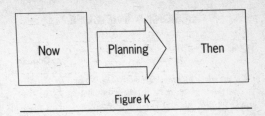

Now | Planning | Then

Figure K

REMEMBER THE PROCESS!

We cannot overemphasize this fact. "Goals, priorities, and planning" are the framework within which to think about your life and to manage it effectively in a way that honors God. Set aside a week during each year in which you will take another inventory and make another assessment of how you are spending your time—managing your life—against the goals that you last set.

Expect your goals to change because you will change. Situations will change. You will make new discoveries. "Forgetting what lies behind . . . press on" (Phil. 3:13-14, RSV).

If you followed the process outlined in this chapter, you've done enough already. If you haven't, why don't you complete the schedule (Figure L) and use this as a planning guide to get under way? Do it now!

TOWARD MORE EFFECTIVE LIVING

There are a good many books on how to be efficient and save time. We've written a few ourselves.[3]

DESIGNING A NEW LIFE

Activity	Done by
1. I will spend four hours alone thinking about what goals I desire for my life and writing down eight short-range goals and eight long-range goals.	
2. I will spend fifteen minutes listing the different ways I am presently spending my time and my own evaluation of them.	
3. I will complete one week of keeping track of all that I do in fifteen-minute increments.	
4. I will take one-half hour to review my calendar or datebook for the past month.	
5. I will spend two hours comparing my desired goals to the way I'm actually spending my life and against my present commitments.	
6. I will analyze the differences between the way I'm spending my time and my present commitments to the way I would like to spend my time.	
7. I will review my life goals in light of this analysis and write new life goals.	
8. I will make a commitment to God, myself, my spouse, and my closest friend to take action.	
9. I will take the first step toward planning life goals.	

Figure L

However, there is a difference between being efficient and being effective. There are three ways to be more effective in the way we use our time:

1. Eliminate things we should not be doing. (They are not our goals.)

2. Do what we should be doing more efficiently.

3. Do the more important things (higher priorities).

YOUR "THINGS-TO-DO" LIST

In the last chapter we talked about the simple technique of just writing down everything you plan to do the next day. This is a very effective way to begin gaining control over your life and time. There are a number of different notebooks that you can get to do this. There is even one notebook available in stationery stores entitled *Dumb Things I Have to Do.* Some desk and pocket calendars have a place to write things that you should do on a particular day.

Many men and women have found it convenient to design their own "Things-to-Do" list and have it mimeographed or even printed to their own specifications. An example of what one person did is given in Figure M. Notice that this individual has followed the very valuable principle of grouping different kinds of events. Experience has shown that most people like things best when they do them in sequence.

TIME-SAVING TIPS

1. *Arrange your environment to fit your goals.* There will always be trade-offs in the amount of time you can invest in doing different things. For example, if you have a lot of brass objects around the house that need to be polished, it might be "cheaper" for you in the long run to have them all polished and sprayed by an expert rather than polishing them yourself. The same would be true of things like yard work.

Essentially, what you are doing is trading off money against hours. But since hours are your life, they are the most important thing!

2. *Use the 80/20 rule.* Vilfredo Pareto was a brilliant Italian mathematician, sociologist, and economist of the last century. He came up with what has come to

be known as the 80/20 rule. Simply stated, it says that "80 percent of the result will come from 20 percent of the events." In church 80 percent of the work gets done by 20 percent of the people; 80 percent of a company's sales come from 20 percent of its products; 80 percent of the outcome of a football game will be the result of 20 percent of the time spent on the field. To put it another way, using our ABC technique, given ten items, only two will be A's.

You can take advantage of this principle by consciously looking for the two opportunities out of ten that will have real payoff, for the two minutes of your time that will save you eight. And reverse the idea: 80 percent of the time that you waste (another way of saying you don't like what you're doing) will be caused by only 20 percent of the things you do. Find those 20 percent and eliminate them.

Apply this principle to your planning. What are the two key steps out of the ten that you have to take that will really bring success? Of the next ten meetings that you are supposed to attend, which two are really important?

3. *Take advantage of delays.* We spend a great deal of time just waiting for things to happen. If you must wait, wait. But don't fret about it. Put the time to work. Pull out your Life Goals Statement and review that. Carry along a book that you always wanted to read. Review your appointment calendar and go over your priorities.

DAILY PLANNING SHEET

Letters to Write

___ Thank-you notes to
___ dinner hosts
___ Don Jones – re/Boston
___ trip
___
___
___

People to see

___ Warren Lutz
___ John Seward
___ George Hann
___
___
___
___

Things to Be Done

___ Draft new project
___ proposal
___ Investigate current procedures
___ for education matls.
___ thank-you notes to hosts
___ memos written on staff
___ mtg.
___ Check out publicity photo
___

Things to Be Planned

___ new billing procedures
___ Budget for new fiscal
___ year to be begun
___
___
___
___

Items to Be Obtained

___ new slide projector
___ extra carousels
___
___
___
___
___

↑   Write priority in this column

Date _____

Phone Calls to Make

___	Ray Baker 798-1233
___	R. Dorney 307/772-4423
___	wife 458-6460
___	A. Yamkin (check up information)
___	new address

Appointments

6:00	
6:30	
7:00	
7:30	
8:00	
8:30	Telephoning
9:00	Dictation, Reading mail etc
9:30	
10:00	
10:30	
11:00	↓
11:30	
12:00	Lunch w/ Bill and Steve
12:30	to discuss budget + billing
1:00	
1:30	Planning time
2:00	
2:30	
3:00	
3:30	
4:00	Free time for others
4:30	
5:00	
5:30	
6:00	
6:30	
7:00	
7:30	Bible Study Fellowship
8:00	Needham's house
8:30	
9:00	
9:30	
10:00	

Figure M

Look at the world around you and find some new thing that you didn't observe before. Strike up a conversation on a positive subject with a person who is also waiting with you. Carry with you a list or post on the wall of your home things you could do in ten minutes: Change the washer in the leaky faucet, clean one drip pan under a stove burner, write a note of appreciation to a friend.

4. *Use strategy when you shop.* Just the act of going to a supermarket consumes a great deal of time. Combine as many purchases as you can to save the time of moving from one store to another. Try to arrange your shopping list in the order in which you know you will move through the supermarket. If you make this a habit, after a while you won't even need the list.

Shop during times when the stores aren't crowded, such as directly after dinner. Carry the current sizes of your children's clothes with you, so that when you see a clothing bargain you can take advantage of it. Buy in quantity whenever you can.

5. *Use strategy when you clean.* Do your sweeping first so that you don't lay dust on tables you've just dusted. Use mats that will pick up the mud at the doors. Stretch out your "spring cleaning" over a number of days by making a list of one thing or one room which you will do on a certain day. Perhaps one day you will shampoo

☞ Checkpoint

Charles Reimnitz, a Lutheran who has presented a number of seminar workshops for professional groups, has focused on "The Dirty Dozen: Time Wasters for Clergymen." Here they are:

1. Personal disorganization
2. Problems with delegation
3. Interruptions
4. Indecision and procrastination
5. Socializing
6. Junk mail and outside reading
7. Lack of planning
8. Television
9. Meetings
10. Family problems and family errands
11. Traveling time and car problems
12. Fatigue

These time wasters pretty well agree with what we have discovered in our own Managing Your Time seminars. Make up your own list and go to work on it!

---

the rugs, and another day, wax the hardwood floors.

Cut down on your laundry time by buying clothes that require little ironing and are colorfast. Read labels on both the clothes and the laundry detergents. Make sure that the family isn't using the laundry hamper as a place to deposit clean clothes rather than hang them up. Ask everyone in the family to find their own clothes after they've been laundered and dried and do their own sorting. On washday have everyone take his own sheets off the bed and put on clean ones.

6. *Take one thing at a time.* Some people seem to be able to accomplish a great deal more than others. What is their secret? Often their approach is to do things one at a time according to their priorities. Doing things one at a time helps them accomplish their tasks much faster than if they tried to do many things at once. In other words, they concentrate, they set priorities and stick to them. Remember—it is not how much we do that counts, but how much we get done!

7. *Learn to set "posteriorities."* Setting individual priorities is simply a matter of deciding what you want to do and when you want to do it. But we also need to set "posteriorities"—deciding what tasks not to tackle and sticking to that decision. You perhaps have noted, as we have, that what you postpone you usually abandon.

8. *Discern God's timing.* We need to be constantly looking for God's timing. Look for that key moment in the lives of others when you can really be God's person, God's helper, to them.

Take time to work—
    it is the price of success.
Take time to think—
    it is the source of power.
Take time to play—
    it is the secret of perpetual youth.
Take time to read—
    it is the fountain of wisdom.
Take time to be friendly—
    it is a road to happiness.
Take time to dream—
    it is hitching your wagon to a star.
Take time to love and be loved—
    it is the privilege of redeemed people.
Take time to look around—
    it is too short a day to be selfish.
Take time to laugh—
    it is the music of the soul.
Take time for God—
    it is life's only lasting investment.

—Author Unknown

Notes

CHAPTER 1

1. Ari Kiev, *A Strategy for Daily Living* (New York: Free Press, 1973), 3.
2. Abraham H. Maslow, *Motivation and Personality* (New York: Harper and Row, 1954). Keith Miller has handled Maslow's concept well in his book, *The Becomers* (Waco, Tex.: Word, 1973).
3. For more about self-esteem, see Dorothy Corkille Briggs's *Your Child's Self-Esteem* (Garden City, N.Y.: Doubleday, 1970).
4. Paul Hersey and Kenneth H. Blanchard, *Management of Organization Behavior* (Englewood Cliffs, N.J.: Prentice-Hall, 1969), 35.
5. We realize when we talk about goals that there is a wide variety of terminology. What we call a *purpose* some people might call a goal, a mission, or an objective. What we call a *goal* others may call an objective, a milestone, a step, or even a standard. But let's not get boxed in by definitions. Accept our terminology for the purposes of this book and then use whatever words for these terms are appropriate in your own setting.

CHAPTER 2

1. For a discussion on delegation and other subjects relating to Christian leadership see Ted W. Engstrom and Edward R. Dayton, *The Art of Management for Christian Leaders* (Waco, Tex.: Word, 1976).

2. C. West Churchman, *The Systems Approach* (New York: Dell Books, 1969).

3. Simon, Howe, and Kirschenbaum, *Values Clarification* (New York: Hart Publishing Co., 1972).

4. For a good discussion on the need to continually review our actions in the light of the Bible and our culture, see Gene Getz's *Sharpening the Focus of the Church* (Wheaton, Ill.: Victor Books, 1984).

5. For a good discussion on the working out of this tension, read Elizabeth O'Connor's *Journey Inward, Journey Outward* (New York: Harper and Row, 1968), the story of the Church of the Saviour, Washington, D.C.

6. For an illustration of the outworking of these three levels of commitment in the life of a local church, read Raymond C. Ortlund's *Lord, Make My Life a Miracle* (Ventura, Calif.: Regal Books, 1974).

CHAPTER 3

1. For a more detailed analysis of problem-solving and its relationship to planning, see Edward R. Dayton's *God's Purpose/Man's Plans* (Monrovia, Calif.: MARC, 1972). See also Charles H. Kepner and B. B. Tregoe, *The Rational Manager* (New York: McGraw-Hill, 1965).

2. Kurt Lewin, *Field Theory in Social Science,* ed. Cartwright Dorwin (Westport, Conn.: Greenwood Press, 1975).

3. If Bud had wanted to read faster, we would have recommended Ben E. Johnson's *Rapid Reading with a Purpose* (Glendale, Calif.: Regal Books, 1973).

4. If you are having trouble in this area, Haim Ginott's *Between Parent and Child* (New York: Avon, 1969) has helped many parents.

CHAPTER 4

1. Psychologists, of course, recognize that many of our conscious and subconscious actions are

rooted in our perception of our past. This is why it is so often necessary for a counselor to lead a person through a review of his or her past and to make peace with the past so that person can move into the future.

2. If this raises more problems than you can handle, try H. Norman Wright's *Communication: Key to Your Marriage* (Glendale, Calif.: Regal Books, 1974).

3. See Edward R. Dayton's *Tools for Time Management* (Grand Rapids, Mich.: Zondervan, 1974), Ted W. Engstrom and Alex MacKenzie's *Managing Your Time* (Grand Rapids, Mich.: Zondervan, 1967), and Alan Lakein's *How to Get Control of Your Time and Your Life* (New York: NAL Books, 1974). One of the "originals" that is still around is Laird's *The Technique of Getting Things Done* (New York: McGraw-Hill, 1947). But remember, all the tools in the world won't help you if you are working toward the wrong goal!

Recommended Reading

Ackerman, Nathan W. *The Psychodynamics of Family Life*. New York: Basic Books, 1958.

Allport, Gordon W. *Becoming: Basic Considerations for a Psychology of Personality*. New Haven, Conn.: Yale University Press, 1955.

————. *Pattern and Growth in Personality*. New York: Holt, Rinehart and Winston, 1961.

Bolles, Richard. *What Color Is Your Parachute?* New York: Crown, 1973.

Churchman, C. West. *The Systems Approach*. New York: Dell Books, 1969.

Dayton, Edward R. *God's Purpose/Man's Plans*. Monrovia, Calif.: MARC, 1972.

————. *Tools for Time Management*. Grand Rapids, Mich.: Zondervan, 1974.

Dobson, James. *Hide or Seek*. Old Tappan, N.J.: Fleming H. Revell,1974.

Drucker, Peter F. *The Age of Discontinuity: Guidelines to Changing our Society*. New York: Harper and Row, 1969.

Engstrom, Ted W., and Edward R. Dayton. *The Art of Management for Christian Leaders*. Waco, Tex.: Word, 1976.

Engstrom, Ted W., and Alex MacKenzie. *Managing Your Time*. Grand Rapids, Mich.: Zondervan, 1958.

Getz, Gene A. *Sharpening the Focus of the Church*. Chicago: Moody Press, 1974.

Ginott, Haim G. *Between Parent and Child*. New York: Avon Books, 1973.

Hersey, Paul, and Kenneth H. Blanchard. *Management of Organization Behavior*. Englewood Cliffs, N.J.: Prentice-Hall, 1969.

Johnson, Ben E. *Rapid Reading with a Purpose*. Ventura, Calif.: Regal Books, 1973.

Johnson, David W., and Frank P. Johnson. *Joining Together*. Englewood Cliffs, N.J.: Prentice-Hall, 1975.

Kennedy, Gerald. *The Lion and the Lamb*. Nashville, Tenn.: Abingdon, 1950.

Kepner, Charles H., and B. B. Tregoe. *The Rational Manager*. New York: McGraw-Hill, 1965.

Kiev, Ari. *A Strategy for Daily Living*. New York: Free Press, 1973.

Lakein, Alan. *How to Get Control of Your Time and Your Life*. New York: Peter H. Wyden, 1973.

Lewin, Kurt. *Field Theory in Social Science*. Edited by Cartwright Dorwin. Westport, Conn.: Greenwood Press, 1975.

Mager, Robert. *Goal Analysis*. Belmont, Calif.: Fearon Publishers, 1972.

Maslow, Abraham H. *Motivation and Personality*. New York: Harper and Row, 1954.

Miller, Keith. The Becomers. Waco, Tex.: Word, 1973.

Mollenkott, Virginia R. *In Search of Balance*. Waco, Tex.: Word, 1969.

Mooneyham, Stanley. *What Do You Say to a Hungry World?* Waco, Tex.: Word, 1975.

Neighbour, Ralph W., Jr. *The Seven Last Words of the Church: We Never Did It That Way Before*. Grand Rapids, Mich.: Zondervan, 1973.

O'Connor, Elizabeth. *Journey Inward, Journey Outward*. New York: Harper and Row, 1968.

Ortlund, Raymond C. *Lord, Make My Life a Miracle*. Ventura, Calif.: Regal Books, 1974.

Osgood, Don. *The Family and the Corporation Man*. New York: Harper and Row, 1975.

Ramm, Bernard L. *The Right, the Good, and the Happy*. Waco, Tex.: Word, 1971.

Reimnitz, Charles. "How Clergymen Use (Misuse) Their Time." *Church Management*, March 1975.

Simon, Sidney, et al. *Values Clarification*. New York: Hart Publishing, 1972.

Slater, Philip E. *Pursuit of Loneliness*. Boston: Beacon Press, 1971.
Wright, H. Norman. *Communication: Key to Your Marriage*. Ventura, Calif.: Regal Books, 1974.

About the Authors

EDWARD R. DAYTON is vice-president-at-large for World Vision International and director of World Vision's Missions Advanced Research and Communication Center (MARC) in Monrovia, California.

Ed is a well-known systems consultant, manager, writer, and lecturer. He holds degrees from New York University and Fuller Theological Seminary and serves on the boards of several international organizations, including INTERDEV, Daystar, and KAIROS. He is the author of more than twenty books.

Ed and his wife, Marge, have four children and seven grandchildren.

TED W. ENGSTROM is president emeritus of World Vision International and former president of Youth for Christ International.

Ted has a broad range of experience in writing, publishing, education, administration, and evangelism. He speaks world-wide on behalf of World Vision and serves as a consultant to churches and businesses. A graduate of Taylor University, Ted is the author of more than forty books, including *Strategy for Living* (Regal Books), coauthored by Ed Dayton. He serves on the boards of twenty organizations, including Focus on the Family and Azusa Pacific University.

Ted and his wife, Dorothy, have three children and five grandchildren.

POCKET GUIDES
NEW FROM TYNDALE

■ *Action Plan for Great Dads* by Gordon MacDonald. A practical look at the essence of leadership in the home. Discover how to build character and confidence in your children. 72-0014-7 $2.25.

■ *The A-to-Z Guide for New Mothers* by Jayne Garrison. Take the worry out of motherhood! Here are suggestions on feeding the baby, assembling a layette, choosing a baby-sitter, and other helpful topics. 72-0008-2 $1.95.

■ *Chart Your Way to Success* by Glenn Bland. Make your dreams come alive with the help of this step-by-step plan tested by thousands of people. Features charts to help you set specific goals. 72-0263-8 $2.25.

■ *Demons, Witches, and the Occult* by Josh McDowell and Don Stewart. Why are people fascinated with the occult? This informative guide will answer your questions about occult practices and their dangers. 72-0541-6 $2.25.

■ *Family Budgets That Work* by Larry Burkett. Customize a budget for your household with the help of this hands-on workbook. By the host of the radio talk show "How to Manage Your Money." 72-0829-6 $2.25.

■ *Getting Out of Debt* by Howard L. Dayton, Jr. At last, a no-nonsense approach to your money problems. Here's advice on creating a budget, cutting corners, making investments, and paying off loans. 72-1004-5 $2.25.

■ *Hi-Fidelity Marriage* by J. Allen Petersen. A respected family counselor shows you how to start an affair—with your own spouse. Learn how to keep love alive . . . rekindle old flames . . . grow from mistakes. 72-1396-6 $1.95.

■ *Increase Your Personality Power* by Tim LaHaye. Why do you get angry? Afraid? Worried? Discover your unique personality type, then use it to live more effectively—at home, on the job, and under pressure. 72-1604-3 $1.95.

■ *Landing a Great Job* by Rodney S. Laughlin. Here are the essentials of a successful job hunt. Everything you need—from finding openings to closing interviews, and accepting offers. 72-2858-0 $2.25.

■ *The Perfect Way to Lose Weight* by Charles T. Kuntzleman and Daniel V. Runyon. Anyone can lose fat—and keep it off permanently. This tested program, developed by a leading physical fitness expert, shows how. 72-4935-9 $2.25.

■ *Strange Cults in America* by Bob Larson. An easy-reading update of six well-known cults: the Unification Church, Scientology, The Way International, Rajneesh, Children of God, and Transcendental Meditation. 72-6675-X $2.25.

■ *Surefire Ways to Beat Stress* by Don Osgood. A thought-provoking plan to help rid your life of unhealthy stress. Now you can tackle stress at its source—and win. 72-6693-8 $2.25.

■ *Temper Your Child's Tantrums* by James Dobson. You don't need to feel frustrated as a parent. The celebrated author and "Focus on the Family" radio host wants to give you the keys to firm, but loving, discipline in your home. 72-6994-5 $2.25.

■ *Terrific Tips for Parents* by Paul Lewis. The editors of *DADS ONLY* newsletter shares his findings on building character, confidence, and closeness at home. 72-7010-2 $2.25.

■ *When the Doctor Says, "It's Cancer"* by Mary Beth Moster. Cancer will strike approximately three out of four American families. Find out how to cope when you or someone you love hears this diagnosis. 72-7981-9 $1.95.

■ *When Your Friend Needs You* by Paul Welter. Do you know what to say when a friend comes to you for help? Here's how to express your care in an effective way. 72-7998-3 $2.25.